BIRCH
BOOKS

First published by Birch Books 2020

ISBN (978-81-949495-2-7)

Email : books.birch@gmail.com

The Fickle Monkey

Ruchira Darda

For my beloved Krishna.

For my mum, who chiseled the best out of me.

For my sons, Aryaveer and Adhiraj,
for sprinkling love and wonder in my life.

Mom asked me the other day,
Why do you wander?
I ask you for water,
But you will sit down to ponder.

One minute,
You are engrossed in a story.
Then, the very next second,
I hear you praising Dori.

I ask you to write,
You will paint.
If I ask you to stop,
You pretend to faint.

If I ask you to colour,
You want to dance.
Then I see you staring at a canvas,
Later, instantly, you take a stance.

I don't get you she said,
And she asked why.
I didn't know how to tell her,
I felt shy.

I looked up at her brown eyes,
Hoping she would break into a smile.
I knew I had to tell her,
I gathered all my courage into a pile.

Mom, I have to confess,
I haven't been honest.
Actually, I really didn't know up until now,
I thought this was a test.

There is a fickle monkey,
Who stays inside of me.
If I say yes,
He says let it be.

When you ask me to sing,
He says go to sleep.
And when you're are about to nap,
He asks me to weep.

The other day,
When you made Mexican rice.
I was thrilled I swear,
It was him who said,
'anything with a little more spice.'

I asked him why,
Why can't you decide.
He said, that's just how I am,
I can't pick a side.

Mom smiled down at me,
Oh! it was such a relief.
Then she shared her secret,
Much to my disbelief.

She whispered in my ear,
I have a fickle monkey of my own.
Before I learnt to tame it,
It sat proud on its throne.

Then one day,
I found the spell.
When I chant my lord's name,
He gets bound by a bell.

Now everytime he comes,
To create mischief and menace.
I am alerted by the bell,
Before he begins his tennis.

Hmm... I thought,
That's all I need to do.
Chant, Chant and Chant ,
To scare off you know who.

Bye folks I got to go,
Before it's too late.
Mom is about to place,
A piece of broccoli on my plate.

The Monkey Inside

1. Do you have a monkey in you?

2. Does he get you into trouble?

3. How do you calm that little monkey?

4. What fun things does that monkey make you do?

5. How do you tell the monkey to take a deep breath?

Pen down your thoughts on each of these characters, how would you describe them?

ABOUT THE AUTHOR

Ruchira Darda is a parent to two inspiring young children. They spend time together weaving stories and exploring the world through them.

Ruchira has a decade of experience working with children via her children's enrichment centre - The Yellow Door. Her pursuit of spirituality is the purpose behind her storytelling. She is an expert on personalities and is a sought after Relationship and Parenting Coach. Her quest for spirituality coupled with her experience with women and children has led her to simplfying her learnings for children.

While she believes spiritual learning should come to children from a young age she also believes that everything we say to our children doesn't need to be so structured. That's why her storytelling is a blend of spurts of laughter, tamed with a dose of goodness.